My First Book about the Animal Alphabet of South America

Amazing Animal Books Children's Picture Books

By Molly Davidson

Mendon Cottage Books

JD-Biz Publishing

Read More Amazing Animal Books

Purchase at Amazon.com

Download Free Books!
http://MendonCottageBooks.com

 **is for an Anteater.**

The Giant Anteater lives in central and south America in grasslands, forests, jungles, and mountains.

They can eat over 30,000 insects per day, their favorite are termites!

B is for a Booby.

Boobies hunt sea fish off the east coasts of Central and South America.

The blue-footed bobby lives in the Galapagos Islands.

C is for a Capybara.

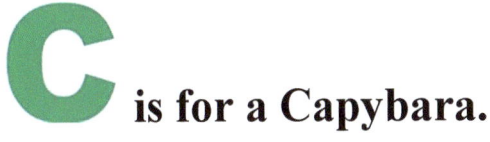

Capybaras live both in water and on land in Central and South America.

After they jump into the water, they can hold their breath for up to 5 minutes.

D is for a Desert Tortoise.

The desert tortoise lives in the deserts of Mexico and South America.

They are pretty small, weighing only about 15 pounds, and measuring about 14 inches.

Their top speed is 0.3 mph (0.5 km/h).

 is for an Emperor Tamarin.

Emperor tamarin monkeys live in the tropical jungles of South America.

It was named after Emperor of Germany, Wilhelm II, whom also had a white mustache.

Babies only live with their mother for 4 - 6 months, before it survives on its own.

F **is for a Flamingo.**

The flamingo is the largest bird in South America, standing up to 5 ft (180 cm) tall.

Flamingoes live in colonies of up to 200 birds, and eat fish and shrimp.

They live between 30 - 50 years in the wild.

G is for a Gila Monster.

It is one of the few venomous lizards in Central and South America.

Their tails will grow to hold more fat, that the Gila monster can use later when they are short on food supplies.

H  is for a Horned Frog.

The horned frog lives in the wetlands of Argentina.

They will try to eat anything that moves near their mouths, mostly insects, birds, lizards, and sometimes other frogs.

I is for an Ibis.

Ibis can be found all over the World, but they prefer the warm swamps, marshes, and wetlands of the southern hemisphere.

Mother ibis lay about 3 eggs per year, and in only a few weeks they hatch, and 6 weeks later the babies will leave the nest.

J is for a Jaguar.

Jaguars are related to leopards, and are the largest cats on the American continent.

Jaguars spend most of their day resting in trees, and love to be close to water, which is rare for a feline.

 **is for a Keel Billed Toucan.**

Toucans live in the tropical jungles of South America, where it stays in holes in trees.

They usually live in flocks with 6 - 15 other birds.

Their beaks can be as long as 7 1/2 in. (20 cm).

L is for a Llama.

Today llamas live mostly in the Andes Mountains of South America.

They were used as pack animals for the ancient Incas, carrying heavy loads. They also ate their meat, and made clothes with their wool and skin.

 **is for a Macaw.**

There are 17 different species of Macaw, which all live in the tropical rainforests of South America.

Many macaws can copy human sounds.

 is for a Nutria.

Nutria, also called Coypu, live in burrows along the warm river banks in the tropics of South America.

Most nutria don't live to be over 3 years old.

There are fur ranches in Asia, North America, Europe, and Africa, which also raise nutria.

 **is for an Ocelot.**

Ocelots, also called painted leopards, live in the jungles of South America.

They are excellent swimmers, but are not very good at climbing or running, like most cats.

P is for a Piranha.

Piranhas live in fresh, quick moving rivers, all over South America.

They have a row of razor sharp teeth, which they use to eat fish, snails, water plants, and any animals they may fall dead into the water.

 **is for a Quetzal.**

The quetzal lives in the tropical rainforests of Mexico, Central and South America.

The boys have bright blue and green body and tail feathers, as well as gold crest feathers on their head.

 **is for a Red Knee Tarantula.**

These burrowing tarantulas live mostly in the mountains of Mexico, Central, and South America.

They can live up to 30 years in the wild!

S is for a Spectacled Caiman.

The spectacled caiman lives in wetlands and rivers all throughout South America.

They are a smaller crocodile only growing to about 6 1/2 feet (2 m) in length, and weighing up to 88 pounds (40 kg).

T is for a Three-Toed Sloth.

The three - toed sloth lives in the trees of Central and South America.

They are known as the slowest moving animals on Earth, moving at a speed of 0.15 mph (0.24 km/h).

 **is for an Umbrellabird.**

![Frank Wouters © Wikimedia Commons]

Frank Wouters © <u>Wikimedia Commons</u>

The umbrellabird, named for its umbrella shaped head crest, lives in the forests of Central and South America

They live high in the trees, until mating season, then they will come down to lower land.

 is for a Vampire Bat.

Vampire bats live in the tropics of Central and South America.

Their body is about the size of a human thumb!

They like to suck the blood of cows, pigs, and tapir, but it doesn't hurt them, since the bats are so small.

W is for a White Faced Capuchin.

The white faced capuchin monkey lives in the tropical forests of northern South America and the southern part of Central America.

They are thought to be the most intelligent monkey, they have been trained to help people that are paraplegic (no movement in their legs).

 **is for an X-Ray Tetra.**

The X-Ray Tetra is a small fish that lives in the Amazon River of South America.

They get their name because they have a clear skin, which lets one see its back bone easily.

 **Y** is for a Yellow - Bellied Siskin.

Gomezprieto © <u>Wikimedia Commons</u>

The yellow-bellied siskin, lives in the mountain oak trees of northern South America.

The boys have a totally yellow belly, but the girls have some olive green on their chests above the yellow.

Z is for a Zorro.

A zorro is a small-eared wolf, which lives in the rainforests of South America, mostly the Amazon Basin.

It is on the Brazilian list of endangered animals, because it is losing its habitat.

Download Free Books!

http://MendonCottageBooks.com

Purchase at Amazon.com
Website http://AmazingAnimalBooks.com

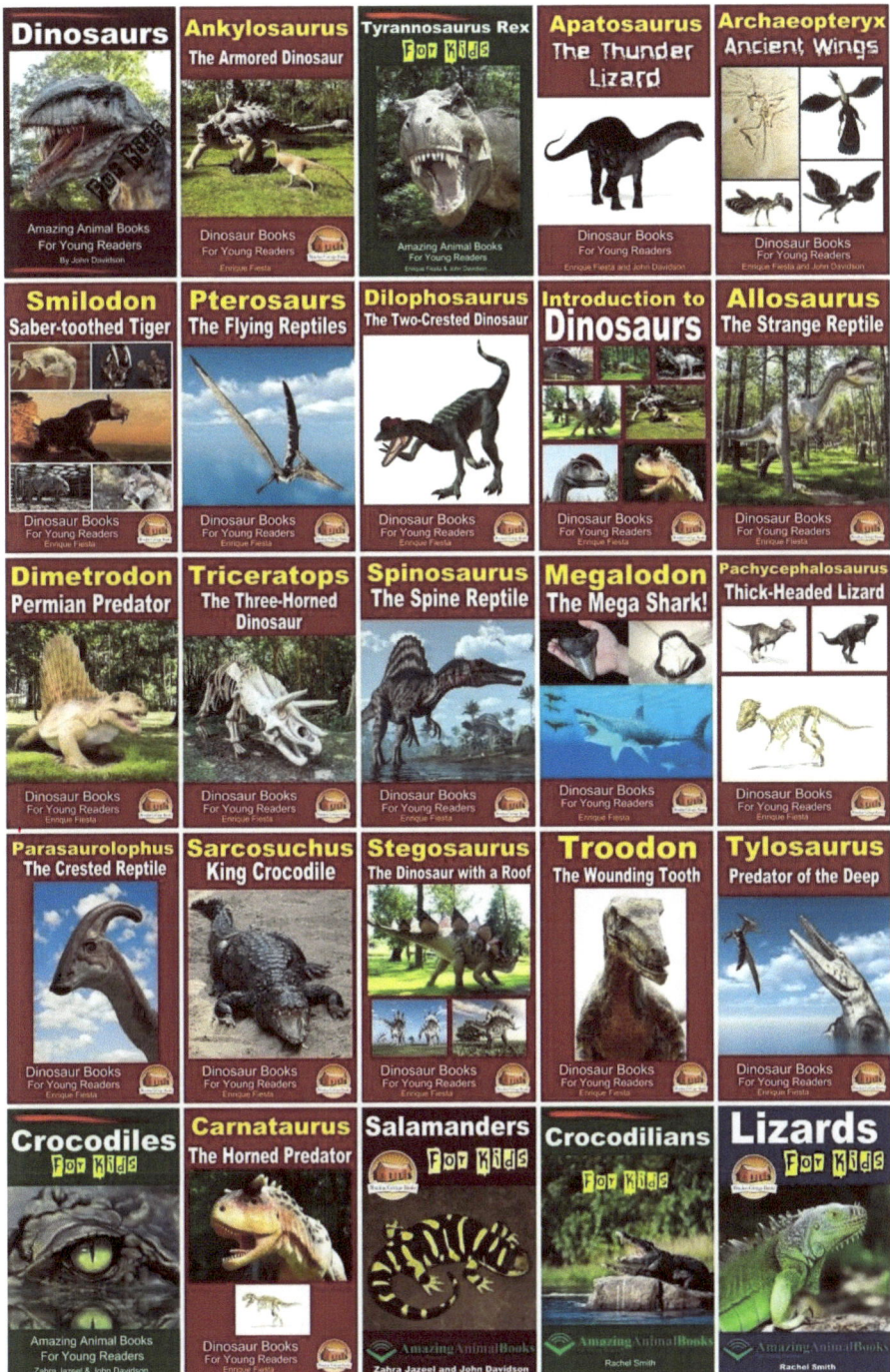

Top Ten Dog Breeds For Kids
Amazing Animal Books For Young Readers
Kisha Bennett & John Davidson

German Shepherds
Dog Books for Kids
K. Bennett

Bulldogs
Dog Books for Kids
K. Bennett

Dachshund
Dog Books for Kids
K. Bennett

Poodles
Dog Books for Kids
K. Bennett

Labrador Retrievers
Dog Books for Kids
K. Bennett

Rottweilers
Dog Books for Kids
K. Bennett

Boxers
Dog Books for Kids
K. Bennett

Golden Retrievers
Dog Books for Kids
K. Bennett

Puppies
Dog Books For Kids
Amazing Animal Books
By John Davidson

Beagles
Dog Books for Kids
K. Bennett

Yorkshire Terriers
Dog Books for Kids
K. Bennett

Dogs
Top Ten Dog Breeds For Kids
Amazing Animal Books For Young Readers
Zahra Jazeel & John Davidson

Cats For Kids
Amazing Animal Books For Young Readers
K. Bennett & John Davidson

Foxes For Kids
Amazing Animal Books For Young Readers
Zahra Jazeel & John Davidson

Wolves For Kids
Amazing Animal Books For Young Readers
By John Davidson and Virginia Fidler

Our books are available at

1. Amazon.com

2. Barnes and Noble

3. Itunes

4. Kobo

5. Smashwords

6. Google Play Books

Download Free Books!
http://MendonCottageBooks.com

Publisher

JD-Biz Corp

P O Box 374

Mendon, Utah 84325

http://www.jd-biz.com/

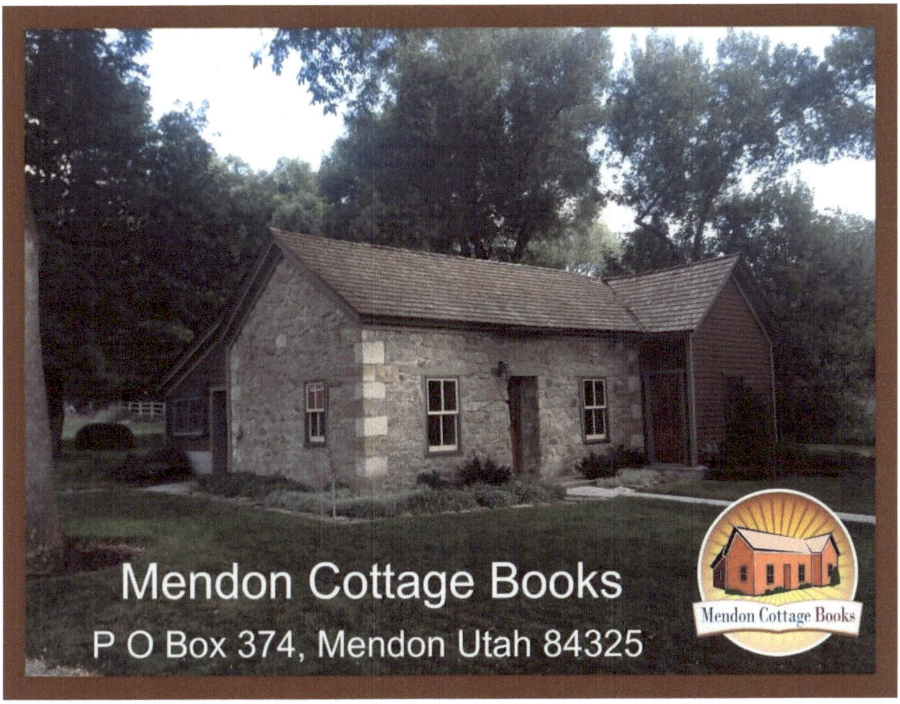

Mendon Cottage Books

P O Box 374, Mendon Utah 84325

www.ingramcontent.com/pod-product-compliance
Lightning Source LLC
Chambersburg PA
CBHW050908290526
45792CB00002B/740